Retro Dos

Illustrations on how to do Vintage Inspired Hair Styles with a Modern Twist.

AuthorHouse™
1663 Liberty Drive
Bloomington, IN 47403
www.authorhouse.com
Phone: 1-800-839-8640

First published by AuthorHouse 05/20/2011

ISBN: 978-1-4634-1454-2 (sc)

Library of Congress Control Number: 2011910024

Printed in the United States of America

This book is printed on acid-free paper.

authorHOUSE®

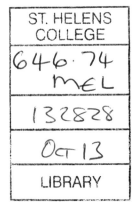

Retro-Dos

is the hairstylist of the past years that is recognized for the height and rolls of her hair-do's. Her fine creations are inspired by the era's we love, the 40's & 50's. Styling for many women across California, Carmela is your retro stylist.

Retro-Dos

Vintage inspired
hair styles with a
modern twist.

by Carmela Melecio

Dedicated to my daughters
Vanessa, Christina and Jessica.

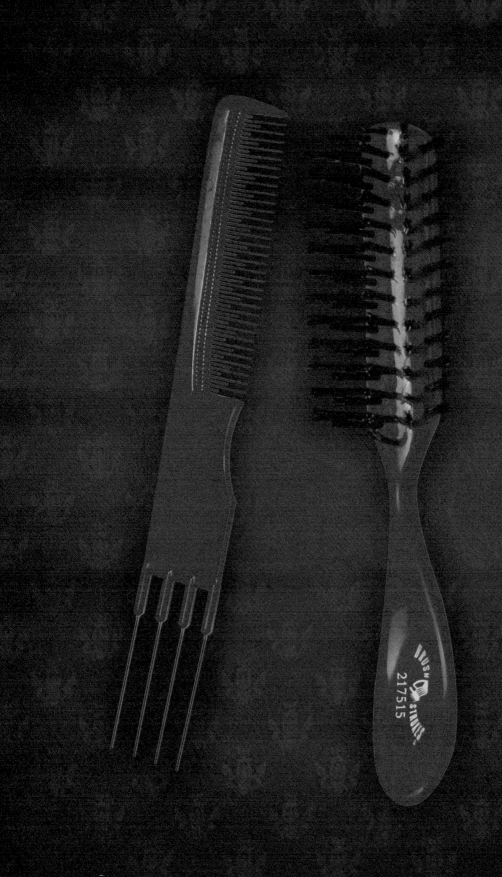

Table of Contents

Special Thanks

To the models & the photographers

Styl·ist [stahy-list]
An artist who is a master of a particular style.
Someone who cuts or beautifies hair.

I've got something special to share with you all, and that's glamorous retro styling with a current twist! I love that retro and vintage look, especially from the 40's and 50's; it inspires me to create beautiful hairdos. I have over 25 years of experience as a hair stylist, and I've done it all, but the passion I have to create retro hair styles is like no other. I love the soft curls, fierce volume, and the way the hair color intensity pops with these styles. It's not only glamorous and sexy, but it's also beautiful art.

In 1979 at the age of 18 I attended Gerard's Beauty Collage in Santa Ana, California. It was there that I learned how to do vintage hair styles from an instructor named Mr. Jenkins. He had mentioned to us that he worked in Hollywood in the 50's and he taught me how to do victory rolls, I liked this form of styling and I wanted to do more, but there wasn't much of a calling for it at the time.

I am blessed with three gorgeous daughters who were part of my dive into the retro world, and what a fabulous world it is! It's fun, glamorous, and craves for current retro styles in hair and in clothing. My creative daughter, Christina, pulled me in with her retro taste in clothing and the two of us became partners in recreating clothing from the 40s and 50s. With our clothing line came along photos shoots and runways, and that's when I began creating my own unique style of retro hair styles. The fabulous pinup model, Ms. Lady Luck, is my daughter Jessica, and as she got her big break into the pinup modeling business, so did my work. Since then I have worked with numerous models, photographers, and magazines, and have appeared at numerous events.

I love taking retro hair styling to another level and creating something modern, current and influenced by the past. Many have asked how I do it and I'd love to share that with all of you.

Therefore, I have put together this step-by-step book on creating some of my hair styles. I promise that "Retro-dos" will lead you in your quest to master the skill of retro hair styling. These styles will take you a few times to master, it takes patients and practice, but then you can create whatever your imagination lets you.

You're going to love these gorgeous hair styles! Good luck and I hope you enjoy this book as much as I enjoyed creating it for you.

Retro-Dos
Carmela Melecio

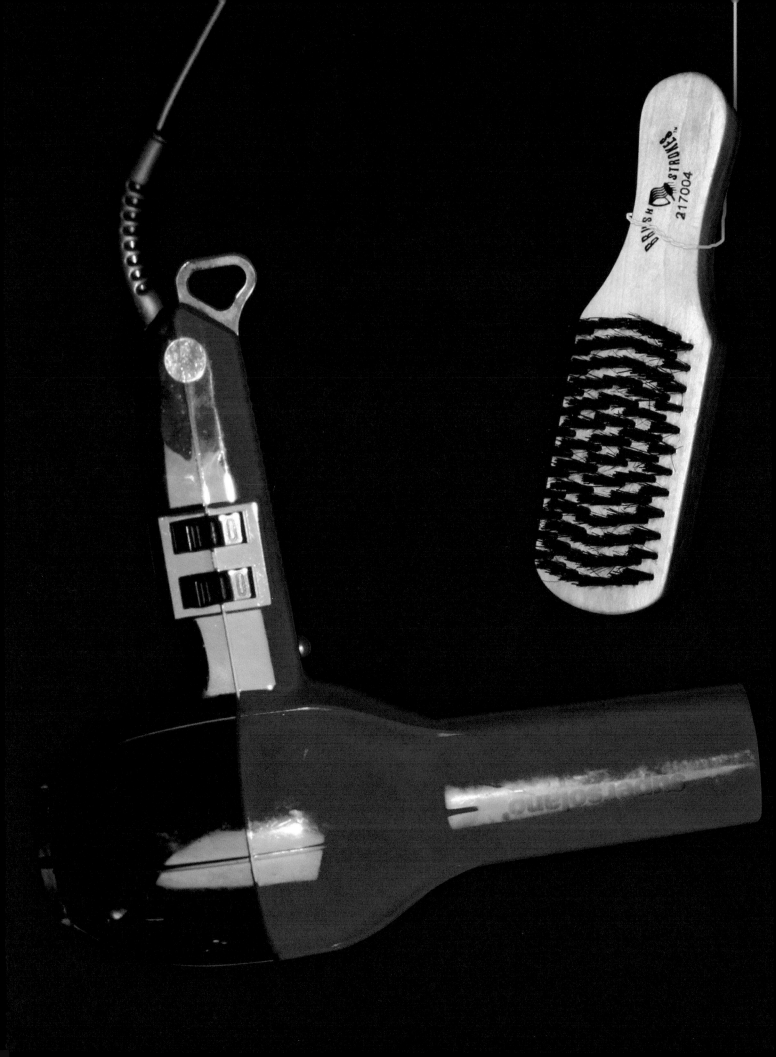

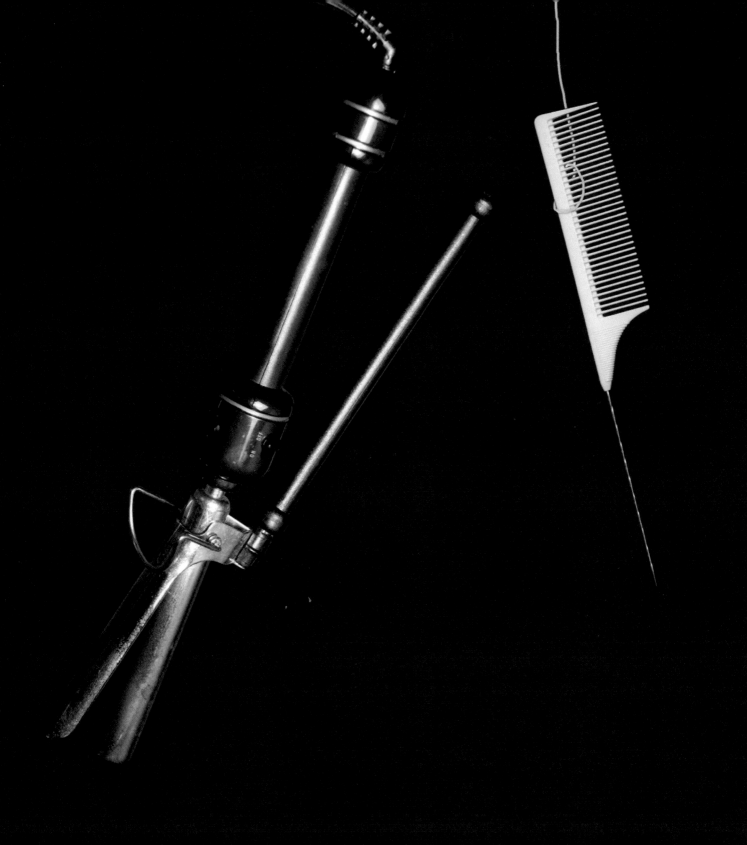

Tools

These are the tool that I use and recommend.
If you prefer to use other tool make sure the result is the same.

Used for parting and sectioning the hair.

Rattail Comb

Backcombing Comb

Used for backcombing the hair. The long thin teeth are used for lifting your roll when shaping.

Used for clipping your curls in place when using the curling iron and for pining sections of the hair out of the way while working on other parts of your hair.

Meta Duckbill Clips

Used for brushing the hair when forming your rolls. It helps to keep the hair smooth. A nylon fiber can also be used.

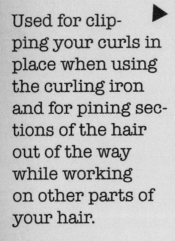
Bobby Pins

Used to hold the hair in place when styling. They come in various colors; try using the color closest to your hair color.

Boar Bristle Brush

Is only used to loosen the curl after the clips have been re-moved.

Vent Brush

Curling Iron

They come in different sizes 3/8 of an inch to 2 inches. For most of my styles I use a 1/2 inch curling iron. Make sure to use hair spray while curling your hair.

Another way to curl your hair. They come in many sizes and work great as well.

Hot Rollers

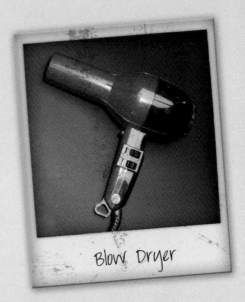

Blow Dryer

I like to use Shaper Plus from Sabastian. It keeps the hair in place without leaving a stiff feel.

Hair Spray

Used for drying fly away ends (hair); getting a clean, finished look.

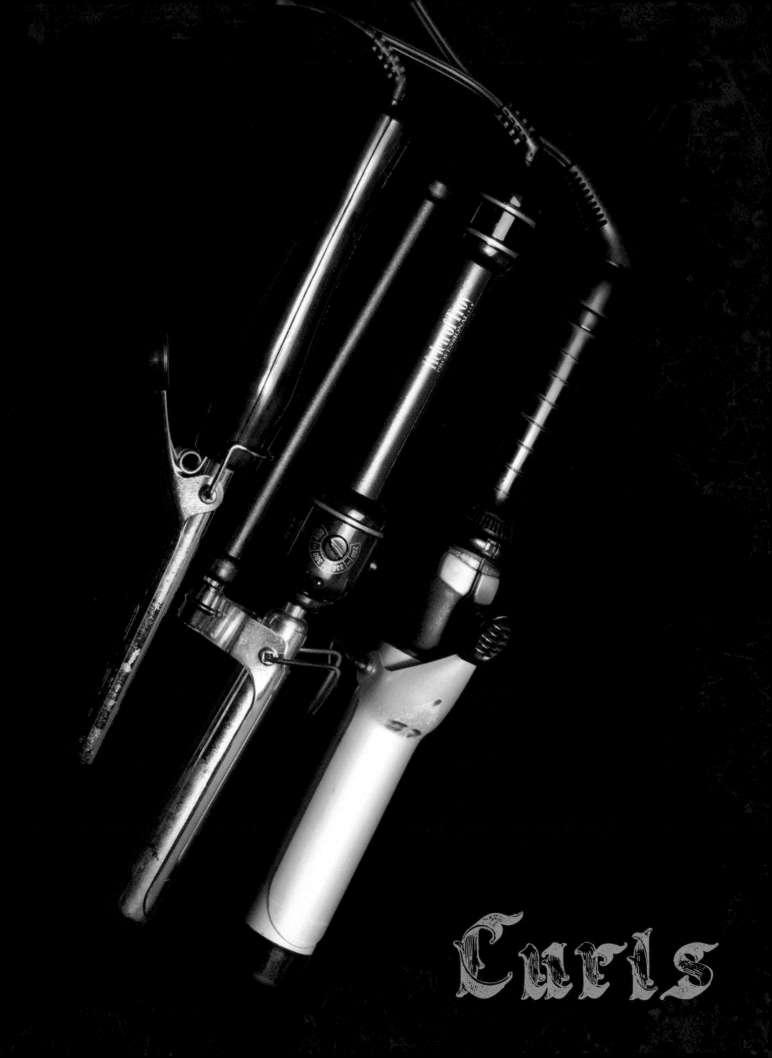

Curls

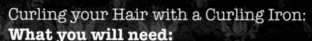

Curling your Hair with a Curling Iron:
What you will need:
1. Rattail Comb
2. Hair Spray
3. Bobby Pins or Duckbill Clips
   - I like to use Duckbill Clips

Starting at the top:
Pick your section of hair and spray it with hair spray. Then roll it back, as seen in picture one. Clip your curl with a bobby pin or Duckbill Clip. Continue to roll all your curls back, proceeding to the sides.

Allow hair to cool once it is all curled and pinned. This helps the curls to last longer.

I use this form of curling for most of my hair styles. This form of curling is done to give body to your hair.

An Important Note:
Make sure all ends of the hair are properly curled, if not you will have fishtails.
Fishtails are bent ends to your hair.

Hot Rollers

Curling your Hair with Hot Rollers:

What you will need:
1. Hot Roller Set
2. Hair Spray

This is great for those who have problems using a Curling Iron. You will roll the hair the same way when using a Curling Iron.

Starting at the top:
Pick your section of hair and spray it with hair spray. Then roll it back, as seen in picture two. Continue to roll all your hair back, proceeding to the sides from the top to the nape.

Allow hair to cool once you are finished. This helps the curls to last longer.

This form of curling is also done to give body to your hair.

An Important Note:
Make sure all ends of the hair are properly curled, if not you will have fishtails.
Fishtails are bent ends to your hair.

Victory Rolls

This is your basic vintage look that many like to use. Once this style is accomplished it is easier to be able to create as many different styles as your imagination lets you.

*

Victory Rolls

1 Lets begin by loosening the curls. Brush lightly with your vent brush. Then with your rattail comb, make a part running straight up from behind the ear on both sides. If you like use a duckbill clip to keep the back section out of the way while you continue.

2 Backcomb the entire front section with your backcombing comb. This is very important, this will determine how big and how firm your roll will be. Make sure that you get close to the root.

3 Once you have backcombed the entire front section, part in two more sections on the top to be able to form two separate rolls. Brush lightly forward to be able to place your bobby pins to form your base. Lay your bobby pins close to the scalp in a crisscross pattern. As shown in picture.

4

Hold the entire piece that you will be using for your roll. Sweep up the piece of hair from just behind the ear and form your roll. Use your Boar Bristle Brush on the outside of your roll to smooth out. Secure with bobby pins as you go. Spray with hair spray and use a blow dryer to get a clean look.

5

Now start with the opposite side the same way, secure with bobby pins in a crisscross pattern and form your roll.

6 While your forming your roll from the right side bring the end of the roll slightly over the front top making it longer then the left side.

7 Try to place the ends of the rolls next to each other, not leaving any space between them. When you get your desired look secure with bobby pins.

8 The best way to clean up fly-aways is to spray with hair spray and before it has time to dry use your blow dryer to dry in any fly-aways. This also gives a really nice finish look.

9 Lower back roll is done in the same manner. Backcomb then brush lightly down, secure with bobby pins in a crisscross pattern. Make sure you secure the pins close to the scalp. Then gather the entire section and brush to smooth.

10 Start rolling inward and secure with bobby pins. Use hair spray and hair dryer to help keep all the hair in place.

11 You can use this style with the roll in the back or just leave the hair down and curled, as shown in picture 11. It all depends on the individual and their preference.

Rockin' Kitty

The Wave

This style has two Victory Rolls with the right side being a bit bigger then the left and joining together giving a wave like look in the front.

*

The Wave

 1

Part hair from right behind the ear all the way over to the other side just behind the ear.

2

Once you have separated your sections clip the back section to keep it out of your way.

 3

Backcomb the entire front section. Make sure that you backcomb the root. You want to have a firm base.

 4

Once you are done backcombing the entire front section, separate in two more sections making your left side a bit smaller then the right.

 5

You start on the left side by brushing it forward then inserting your bobby pins with crisscross pattern to form your base.

6

Pick up your entire piece and brush the outside with your Boar Bristle Brush to smooth.

7

Sweep up and twist to form your roll and pin with bobby pins to hold in place.

8

While forming the smaller roll when you reach the top leave it unfinished so you can use it to blend with the other side.

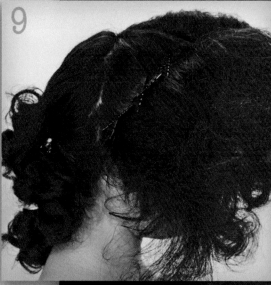

9 Start the other side the same way, place your bobby pins in a crisscross pattern. Then brush the outside with your brush to smooth.

10 Remember that when you are forming the roll on the left side it should be slightly bigger then the right side, Give yourself more hair to work with. Once you have reached the top front part of your roll and you start to finish it, bring the unfinished part on the opposite side and blend it in.

11 Once you have blended the rolls together use your hair spray and blow dryer to clean up any fly-aways, giving you a nice clean look.

12 Styling the back can be left down with curls, as shown in the picture.

13 Styling the back like picture 13. Brush all the hair from the back to your right side of your head and insert bobby pins to hold hair in place. Overlap your bobby pins to have a firm grip. Fluff the curls and spray for that finish look

Gia Genevieve

Vintage Twist

This style consists of two Victory Rolls on each side gathering in the back with a pony-tail look & small curls on the bangs

*

Vintage Twist

1 You start with rolling the entire hair back with the exception of the bang area. Use a 3/8 of an inch curling iron on the bangs. Try to make them very small.

2 Part the hair from the top center of the head to behind the ear, about 2 inches below the ear. Do this on both sides.

3 Backcomb the entire front section except for the small curls that are on the bangs. Make sure that the backcombing is close to the scalp.

4 Make sure that you brush down the back section and pin with a duckbill clip to keep out of the way.

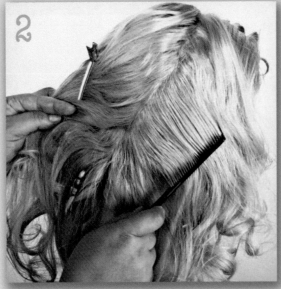

5 Brush lightly forward and pin with bobby pins with a crisscross pattern to form your base. Do this on both sides.

6 Hold the entire piece that will be rolled. Sweep up the piece of hair from just behind the ear and form your roll. Use your Boar Bristle Brush on the outside of your roll to smooth. Secure with bobby pins as you go.

7 Spray with hair spray and use blow dryer to help form a clean roll.

8 Start the other side the same way. Pick up the entire piece and sweep up into your roll and insert your bobby pins to secure.

9 Once you have formed both Victory Rolls, backcomb your bangs with your Backcombing Comb fluff and separate the small curls.

10 For the lower back, make sure all the hair is brushed down flat against the head and secure at the nape with bobby pins in a crisscross pattern

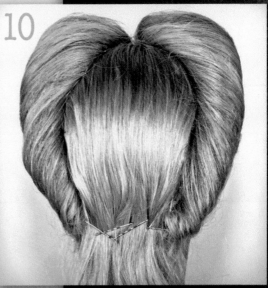

11

12

13

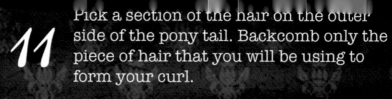

11 Pick a section of the hair on the outer side of the pony tail. Backcomb only the piece of hair that you will be using to form your curl.

12 After you backcomb the root, make your curl rolling upward and insert bobby pins to secure.
Note: Try to place the curl over the pins that are at the base.

13 Form your other curl on the opposite side in the same manner. Remember to try to hide the pins that are on the base. Finish by spraying with hair spray and using your blow dryer to clean any fly-aways.

Bumper Bang

This style consist
of a victory roll that
runs across
the front
in the
bang
area.

*

Bumper Bang

1. Section off the hair by making a part from just behind the ear all the way across to the other ear. As shown on picture.

2. Place duckbill clips to hold the back hair out of the way. Backcomb the entire front section making sure that you get close to the root.

3. Brush the top of the sectioned hair flat down against the head and place bobby pins close to the scalp in a half circle pattern. As shown in picture. Spray the flat section with hair spray to make sure your base is firm.

4 Start on one side, bring the hair strait up and twist inward and insert bobby pin to secure.

5 Continue to roll inward on each side to form two barrels, add bobby pins as needed to secure. You should have two barrels as seen in picture.

6 Gather the ends of the two barrels and bring them up and brush the outside of the roll with your boar bristle brush to smooth.

11 Roll up and inward to connect the two rolls together. You want to bring in and pinch and insert as many bobby pins as needed to form your barrel.
Note: This takes some practice. You want to make sure that it is smooth and clean.

12 You want your roll to look solid all across the front bang area. Use the back of the backcombing comb to help form our roll.

13 Once you are done with your roll, clean up any fly-aways with your hair spray and blow dryer for a finish look.

Ms Lady Luck

The Tube Bang

This Style consist of a Victory
Roll shaped in a "U" in front
in the bang area .

*

The Tube Bang

1 Section off the hair by making a part from just behind the ear all the way across to the other ear as shown in the picture.

2 Place Duckbill Clips to hold the back hair out of the way. Backcomb the entire front section making sure that you get close to the root.

3 Brush the top of the sectioned hair flat down against the head and place bobby pins close to the scalp in a half circle pattern; as shown in the picture. Spray the flat section with hair spray to make sure your base is firm.

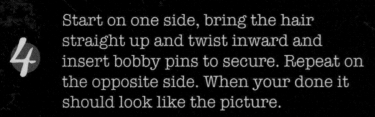

4 Start on one side, bring the hair straight up and twist inward and insert bobby pins to secure. Repeat on the opposite side. When your done it should look like the picture.

5 Continue to roll inward on each side to form two barrels, add bobby pins as needed to secure. You should have two barrels as seen in picture.

6 Gather the ends of the two barrels and bring them up and brush the outside of the roll with your Boar Brush to smooth.

7 Roll up and inward to connect the two rolls together. You want to bring in and pinch and insert as many bobby pins as needed to form your barrel.
Note: This takes some practice. You want to make sure it is smooth and clean.

8 You want your roll to look like a "U". Insert bobby pins between the two barrels to connect them together.

9 Once you are done with your roll, clean up any fly-aways with your hair spray and blow dyer for a finished look.

Add Barrel Curls

1 To style the back with barrel curls, gather all of the hair in a Pony Tail. Make sure it is smooth.

2 You want four pieces to make four separate big Barrel Curls. Pick up one piece and backcomb it at the root then brush with your Boar Bristle Brush to get a smooth look and form your roll.

3 This is where your own creativity comes in. Place your curls as you desire. You want to make sure that you place your Barrel Curls close to each other. Use your bobby pins to secure the hair in place.

Tip: Once you have created your look you could add flower to finish the look.

Neva Moore

54

The Edsol

This style has two Victory Rolls
which join in front with one
curl in the center.

*

The Edsol

1 Make a part from the top of the head to behind the ear on both sides. Clip the back of the hair with a Duckbill Clip to keep it out of the way.

2 Backcomb the entire front section leaving a small section in the very front. Make sure you backcomb close to the scalp.

3 Once you have done the backcombing, brush forward close to the scalp and place bobby pins in a crisscross pattern. Do this on both sides. Make sure that the pins are close to scalp.

4 Slightly brush with your Boar Bristle Brush to smooth the outside of the roll and sweep up the section of the hair from just behind the ear. Secure with bobby pins as you form your roll bring it all the way up to the top and finish it with a nice smooth curl. Spray with hair spray to clean any fly-aways.

5 Once you have made the first roll make sure to leave the front section with enough hair to make your roll at the end.

6 Make sure to spray with hair spray as you go along and use your blow dryer to clean up any fly-aways.

7 Start the other roll the same way. Brush the outside to smooth then sweep up and insert your bobby pins to secure the hair in place.

8 Once you have created your two rolls, backcomb your small bang section then brush slightly to smooth. Then form your barrel curl right in the center of your two Victory Rolls.

9 For the back brush the hair straight down against the head. Firmly place bobby pins to secure the hair, making sure that the pins are secure against the scalp. To form a firm base spray with hair spray.

10 Pick up a piece of hair and backcomb individual pieces and fluff with the back of your Backcombing Comb.

11 Once you have fluffed up the curls, Try to place curls over bobby pins to hide them, as seen in the picture. Finish with hair spray.

Erica Vaughn

The Big Barrel Roll

This is mainly one big roll in the center of the head with smaller curls in the back.

*

The Big Barrel Roll

Loosen your curls with a vent brush, this just separates the curls.

Make your part from behind the ear all the way to the other side, behind the ear. This part is lower so it should be about 6 inches from the top of your head. Make the top half section bigger then the bottom half

Clip the hair back with a Duckbill Clip to keep away as you work on the top half. Backcomb the entire top section. Make sure that you get down to the root. That will ensure that you get a big firm roll on the finial look.

Grab the entire top section and brush with your Boar Bristle Brush to smooth all the hair to the left of the head. Brush firmly against the head.

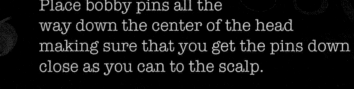

6 Place bobby pins all the way down the center of the head making sure that you get the pins down close as you can to the scalp.

Note: The pins are not n a crisscross section they are more straight just over lapped to get a more secure hold.

8 Hold the piece of hair that you are going to roll and brush to smooth.

9 Start to roll the hair upward and inward to the top of the head.

10 Make sure to cover the bobby pins that you have at the base. Once you have it where you want, Start by inserting your bobby pins to hold the hair in place. Spray with hair spray and use blow dryer to help form a clean roll.

11 Once your roll is done, it should look like the picture shown.

12 You want to have your roll in the center, as shown in the picture.

13 To style the bottom half just pick up a piece of hair and backcomb slightly at the root and form your Barrel Curl insert your bobby pins. Once again your own creativity comes in. You place the curls as you see it and then pin them up.

14 Once you have your desired look, spray your do with hair spray and use your blow dryer to clean up and fly-aways.

Kira Von Sutra

Chris Gomez
PHOTOGRAPHY

Alvarado

Rockin Kitty

Alvarado

71

Styl·ist [stahy-list]

An artist who is a master of a particular style.
Someone who cuts or beautifies hair.

Good luck in your journey of styling.

All the images in the demonstrations where taken
by Lucky Me Photography, and all photos were
edited by RetroSpeck Design, Jessica Melecio.

Special thank you to all the models that
helped with this book,

Cathy Garcia
Gia Genevieve
Kiti Kobain
Ms Lady Luck
Neva Moore
Eria Vaughn
Kira Von Sutra

Like to thank the following models for their
images in the Montage Pages

Christine Fury
Devine Marie
Ms Lady Luck
Pheenix Van Sparks
Cathy Garcia
Vivi Louise
Kimmie Caracoles
Britt Honey
McKensie Westmore

Special thank you to the photographers that
shared their amazing images

Robert Alvarado
Miss Missy Photography
Michele Muerte Photo Graphics
Photosmithography
Girlie Show Photography
Chris Gomez
Robert Venerable
RP Photography

For more hairstyles check out www.dollfacedesign.com

Designed by RetroSpeck Designs,
Jessica Melecio

CPSIA information can be obtained
at www.ICGtesting.com
Printed in the USA
LVIC07n1419110913
352005LV00044B

* 9 7 8 1 4 6 3 4 1 4 5 4 2 *